WITH CD

PIANO *Adventures*®

Challenging pieces with changing moods and changing hand positions

by Nancy and Randall Faber

THE BASIC PIANO METHOD

Production: Frank J. Hackinson
Production Coordinator: Philip Groeber
Editor: Edwin McLean
Cover: Terpstra Design, San Francisco
Engraving: Tempo Music Press, Inc.

FABER
PIANO ADVENTURES®

ISBN 978-1-61677-602-2

Table of Contents

("Gold Star" characteristics of each piece)
Color the star gold or put a star sticker for each piece you learn!

FF1602

Page		Vocal/Instrumental CD Track	Piano CD Track

CD Instr. 1   Piano 2

I Found a Penny

Words by Crystal Bowman
Music by Nancy Faber

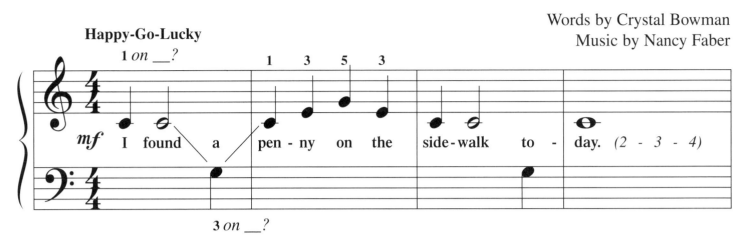

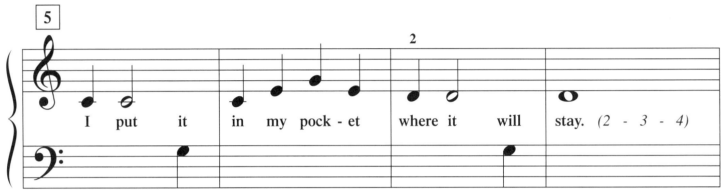

Teacher Duet: (Student plays 1 octave higher)

FF1602

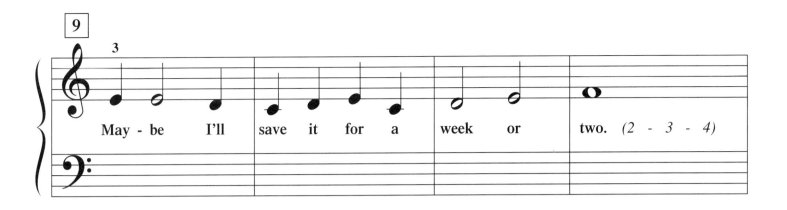

9

3

May - be I'll save it for a week or two. *(2 - 3 - 4)*

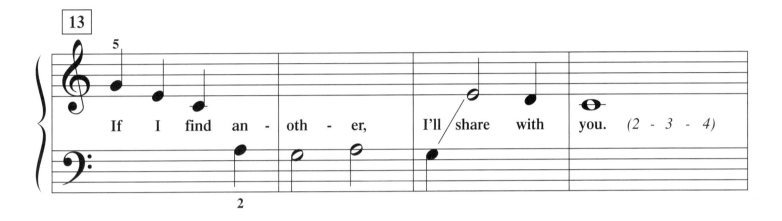

13

5

If I find an - oth - er, I'll share with you. *(2 - 3 - 4)*

2

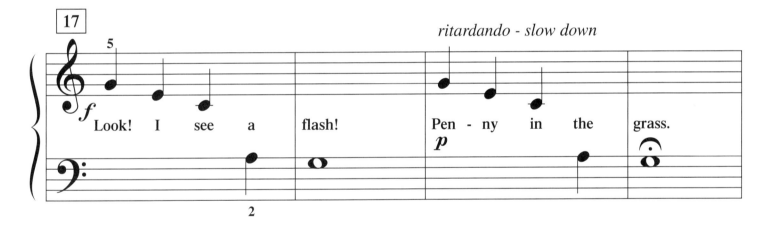

17

5

ritardando - slow down

f Look! I see a flash! Pen - ny in the grass.

p

2

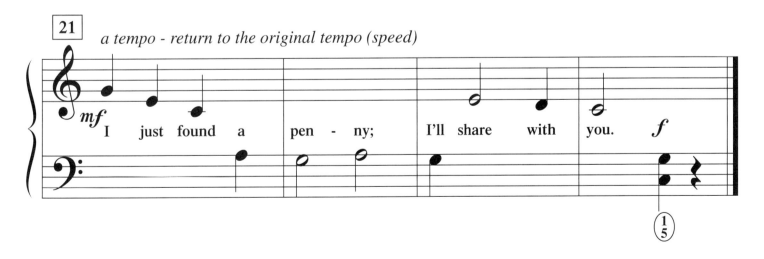

21

a tempo - return to the original tempo (speed)

mf I just found a pen - ny; I'll share with you. *f*

$\binom{1}{5}$

DISCOVERY Where are *measures 13-16* repeated later in the piece? What is new at the very end? Tell your teacher.

CD Instr. 3 Piano 4

Pterodactyls, Really Neat

Words by Jennifer MacLean
Music by Nancy Faber

Play BOTH HANDS 2 octaves LOWER than written.

Stomping heavily

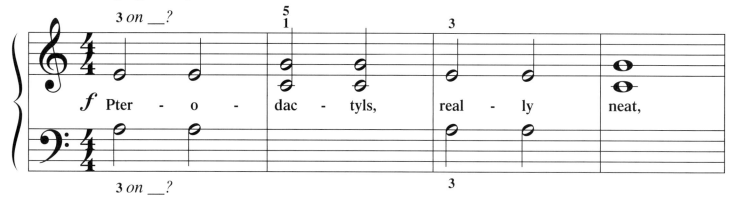

Pter - o - dac - tyls, real - ly neat,

Great wide wings——— and tal - oned feet.

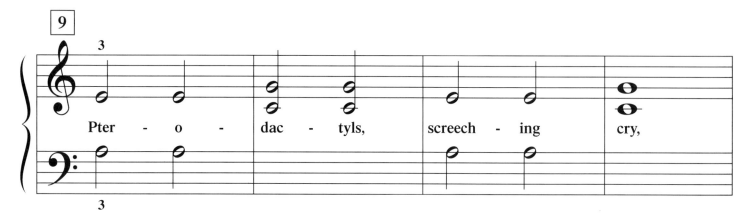

Pter - o - dac - tyls, screech - ing cry,

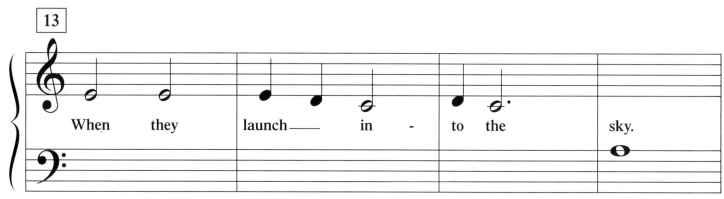

When they launch——— in - to the sky.

FF1602

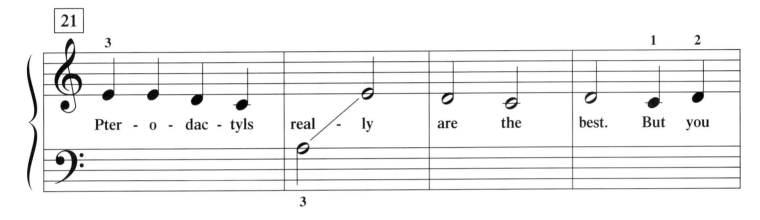

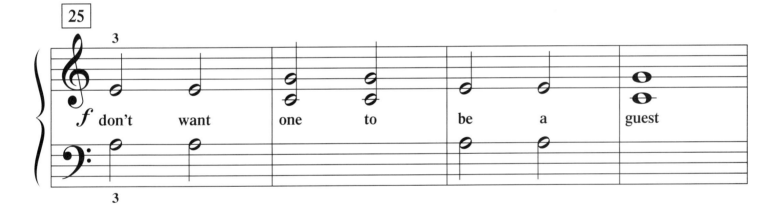

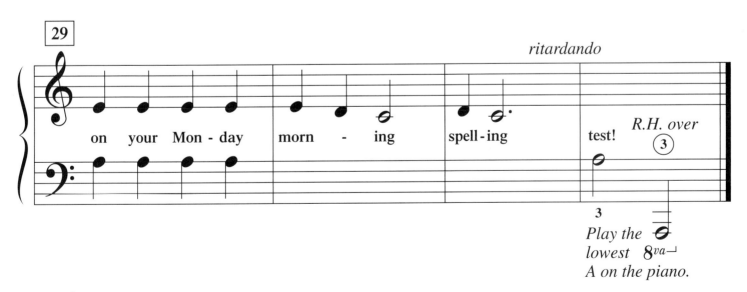

ritardando

R.H. over ③

Play the 𝅝 *lowest* **8**ᵛᵃ⌐ *A on the piano.*

DISCOVERY Where does the *first* line of music return later in the piece? Tell your teacher. Hint: It returns two times.

CD Instr. **Piano**

Zoom, Zoom, Witch's Broom

**Hold the damper pedal
down throughout the piece.**

Words by Jennifer MacLean
Music by Nancy Faber

Zipping along

Zoom, zoom, witch-'s broom!

See her fly a - cross the moon. Fly, fly,

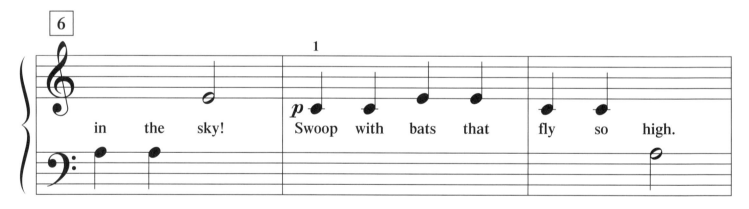

in the sky! Swoop with bats that fly so high.

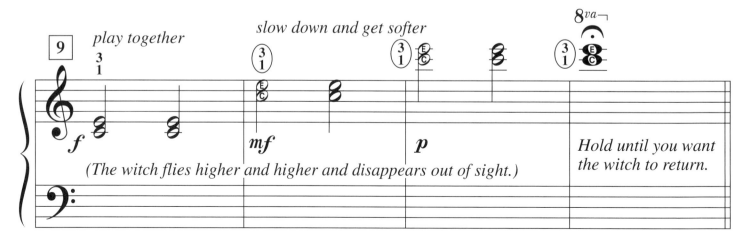

play together

slow down and get softer

(The witch flies higher and higher and disappears out of sight.)

*Hold until you want
the witch to return.*

FF1602

13 Scream, scream, hair so green!

15 *p* I can't wait till Hal - lo - ween!

17 *f* Zoom! *mf* Zoom! *p* Zoom! *pp* (very soft)

DISCOVERY This piece uses **3 letter names** from the musical alphabet. Can you name them?

③ *Play the lowest A on the piano.*

Teacher Duet: (Student plays as written, without pedal)

Theme and Variations

Words and Music
by Nancy Faber

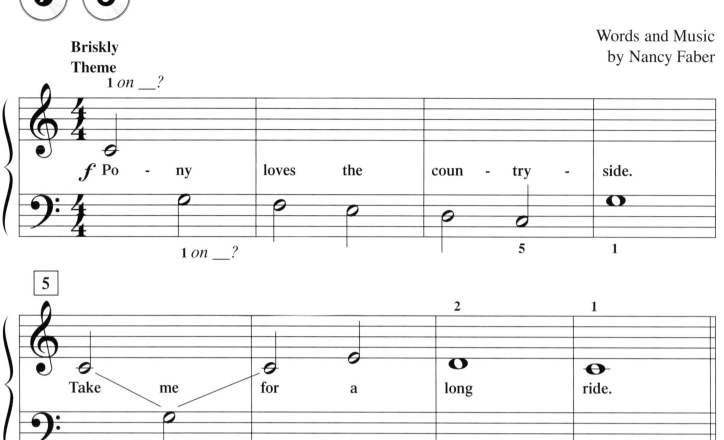

Briskly
Theme

1 *on* __?

f Po - ny loves the coun - try - side.

1 *on* __?

Take me for a long ride.

Teacher Duet: (Student plays 1 octave higher)

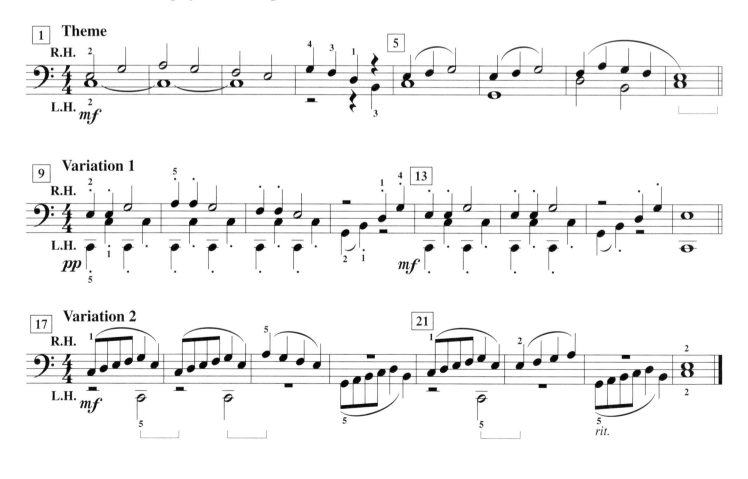

1 **Theme**

9 **Variation 1**

17 **Variation 2**

rit.

FF1602

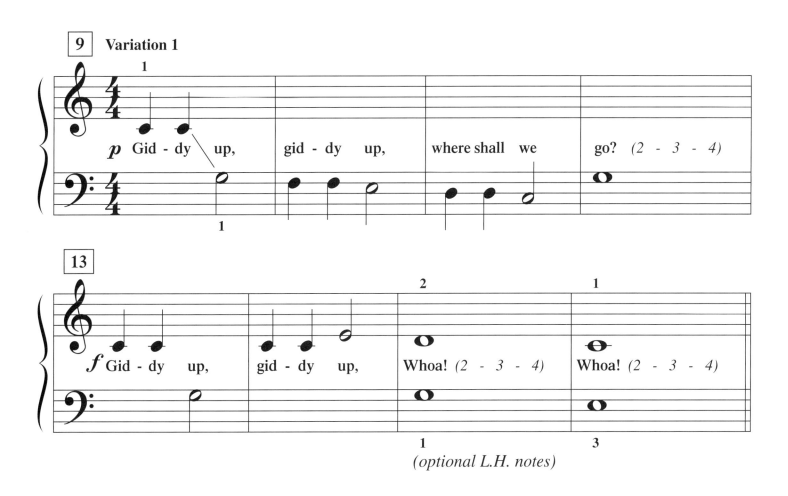

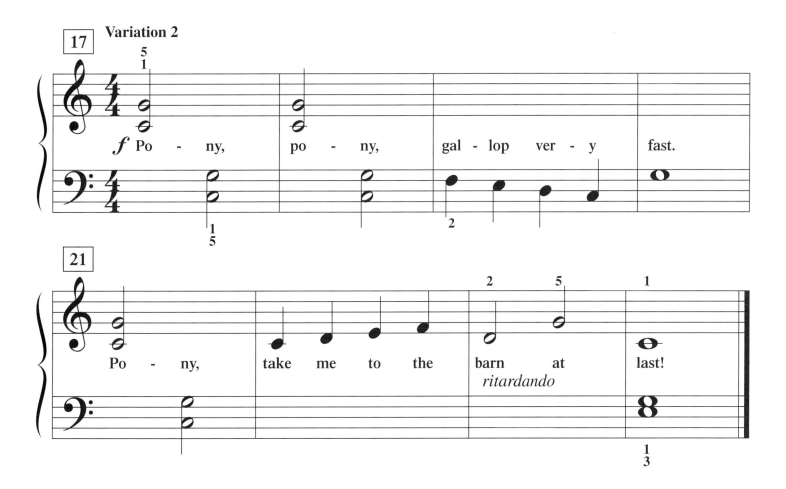

DISCOVERY

Which **variation** is your favorite? Tell your teacher why.

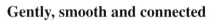

A Rainbow Is a Smile
(Turned Upside Down)

Words by Crystal Bowman
Music by Nancy Faber

Gently, smooth and connected

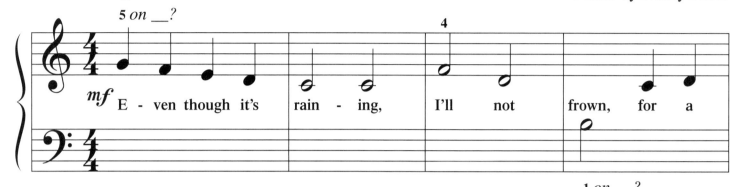

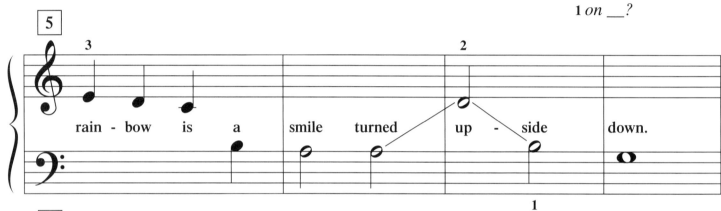

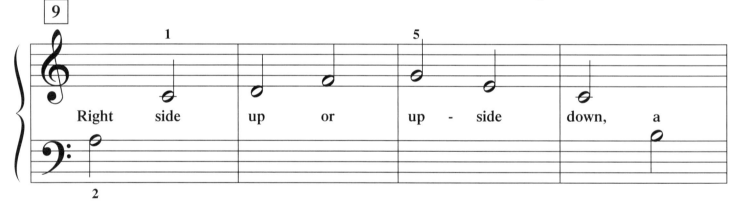

Teacher Duet: (Student plays 1 octave higher, without pedal)

FF1602

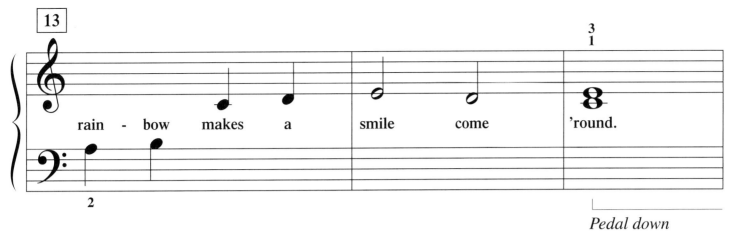

rain - bow   makes   a   smile   come   'round.

Pedal down

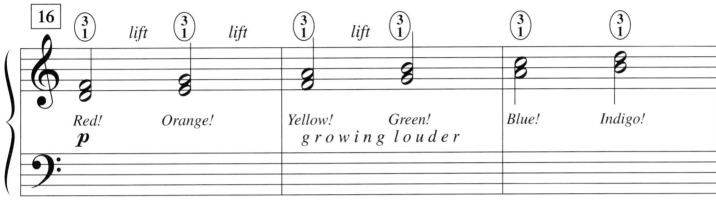

Red!   Orange!   Yellow!   Green!   Blue!   Indigo!
p   *g r o w i n g   l o u d e r*

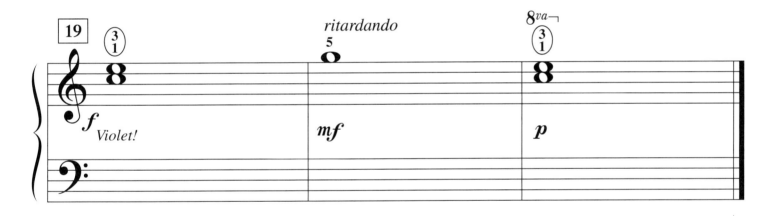

ritardando

8va

f Violet!   *mf*   *p*

Lift pedal.

DISCOVERY

Hold the pedal down and play 3rds *high* on the piano. Listen to the ringing sounds!

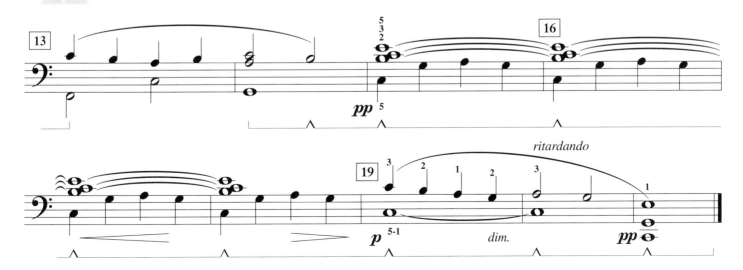

ritardando

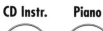

Hello to the Drum

Words by Crystal Bowman
Music by Nancy Faber

Strong march beat

Teacher Duet: (Student plays 1 octave higher)

FF1602

9

Clar - i - nets can play a song, but I have to say, "Hel -

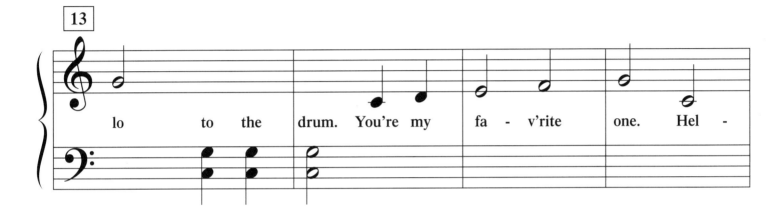

13

lo to the drum. You're my fa - v'rite one. Hel -

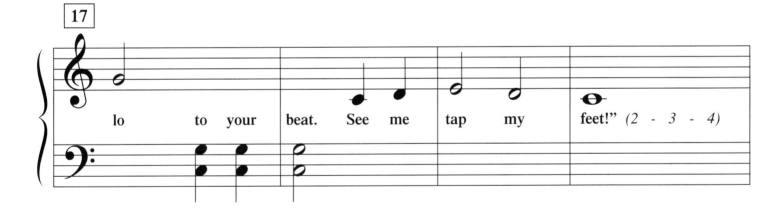

17

lo to your beat. See me tap my feet!" *(2 - 3 - 4)*

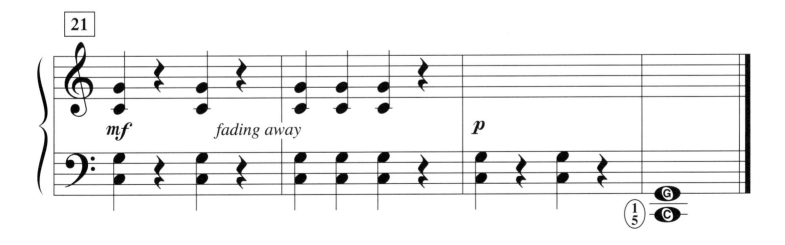

21

mf   *fading away*   *p*

DISCOVERY

Where is the **introduction** and **coda** (special ending) in this piece?

Pony Express

Words and Music
by Nancy Faber

Riding swiftly

3 *on* __?

Po - ny on the snow - y moun - tains, in the for - ests,

3 *on*
__?

on the plain. Car - ries mail a - cross the coun - try

through the wind and rain. Po - ny and his

(Move to the C 5-finger scale.)

rid - er, mail bag on each side.

(Return L.H. to Middle C Position.)

FF1602

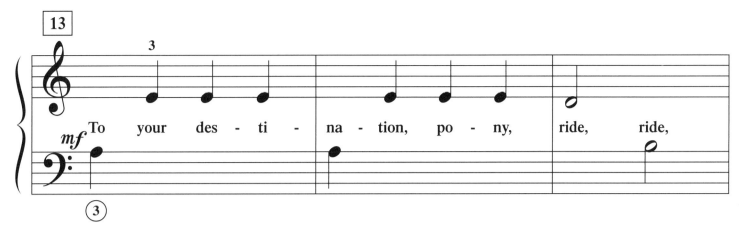

13

To your des - ti - na - tion, po - ny, ride, ride,

③

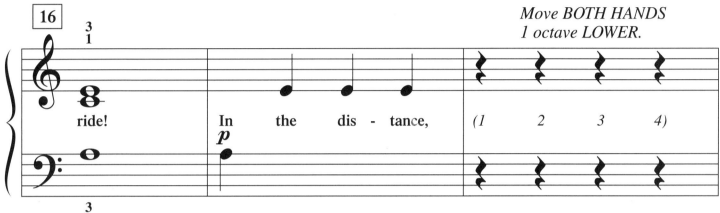

16

Move BOTH HANDS
1 octave LOWER.

ride! In the dis - tance, (1 2 3 4)

③

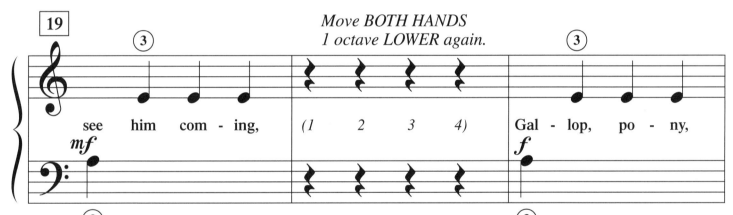

19

Move BOTH HANDS
1 octave LOWER again.

see him com - ing, (1 2 3 4) Gal - lop, po - ny,

③ ③

8*va* BOTH HANDS ⌐ — — ┐
(1 octave lower)

15*ma* BOTH HANDS — — — —
(2 octaves lower)

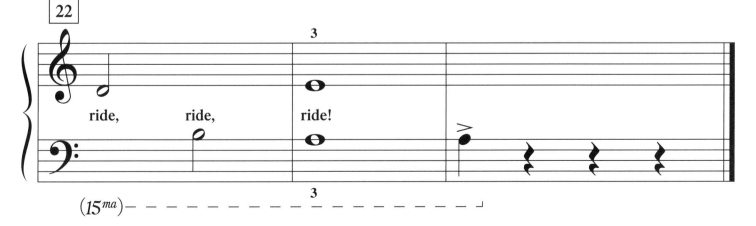

22

ride, ride, ride!

(15*ma*) — — — — — — — — — — ┐

DISCOVERY

Where is there an *accent* in this piece?
Can you brace your L.H. finger 3 with the thumb as you play it?

Cartoon Stories
1. Clown Car

CD Instr. 15 Piano 16

Nancy Faber

Zooming along

Teacher Duet: (Student plays 1 octave higher)

FF1602

**Hold the damper pedal
down throughout the piece.**

2. Parakeet Waltz

CD Instr. 17 Piano 18

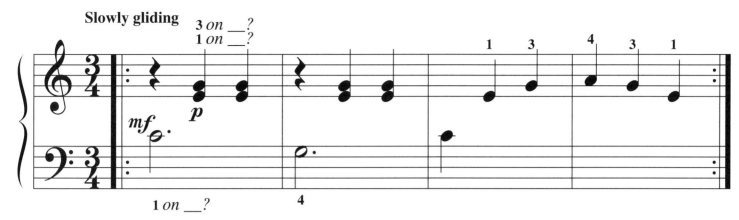

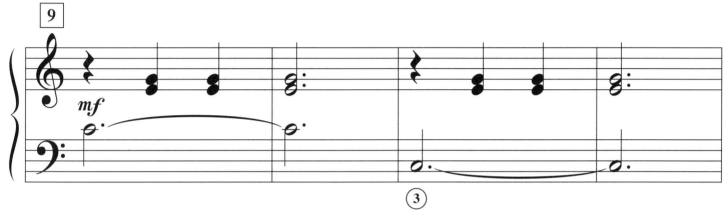

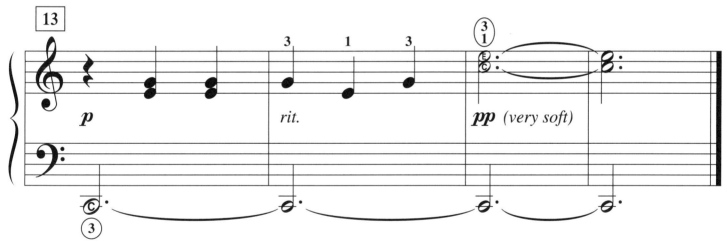

Teacher Duet: (Student plays as written)

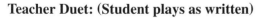

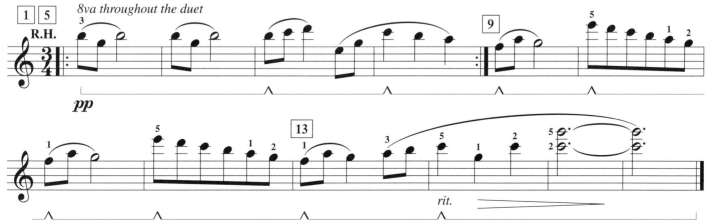

3. Bananappeal

Teacher Duet: (Student plays 1 octave higher)

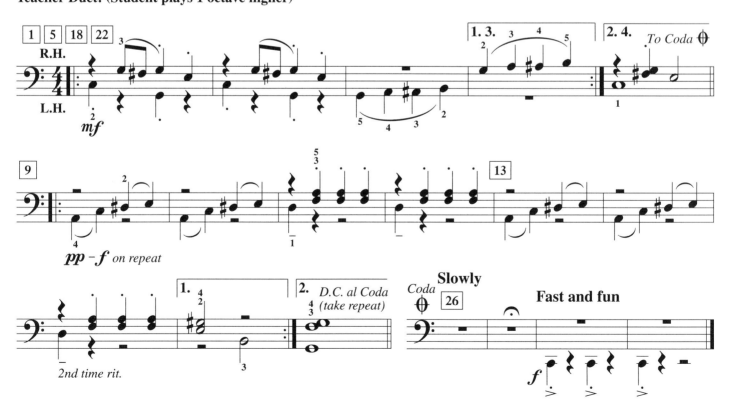

FF1602

Bluebird on My Shoulder
Secondo

U.S. Folk song
Adapted by Nancy Faber

Play as written.
Happily

FF1602

Bluebird on My Shoulder
Primo

U.S. Folk song
Adapted by Nancy Faber

A Particularly Pleasing Piano Piece

Words by Jennifer MacLean
Music by Nancy Faber

Happily

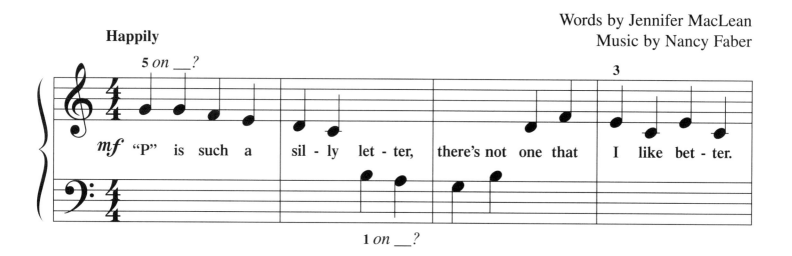

5 on __?

mf "P" is such a sil - ly let - ter, there's not one that I like bet - ter.

1 on __?

5

"P" goes pop, it's sure to please! Let's pick out words that start with "P."

9 Move to the 2-black keys.

(one octave higher)

8va

R.H.

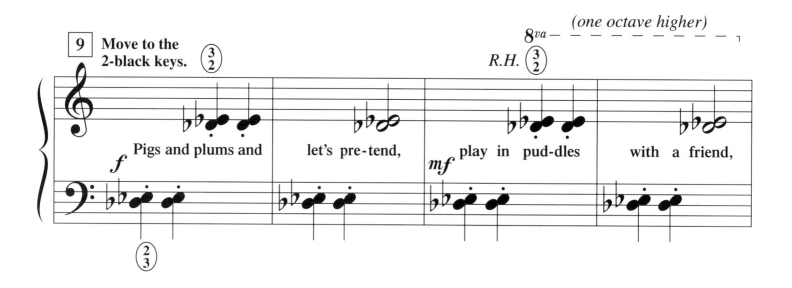

f Pigs and plums and let's pre-tend, mf play in pud-dles with a friend,

FF1602

DISCOVERY

Point out 3 measures that have the **quarter rest**.

Squinchy-Pinchy Shoes

Words by Jennifer MacLean
Music by Nancy Faber

FF1602

CD Instr. 27 Piano 28

French Cathedrals

**Hold the damper pedal
down throughout the piece.**

French Folk song
Arranged by Nancy Faber

Joyfully

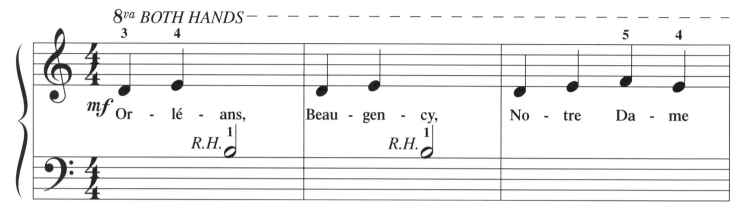

8va BOTH HANDS

mf Or - lé - ans, Beau - gen - cy, No - tre Da - me

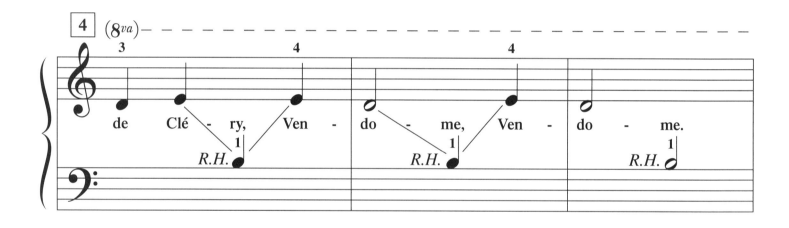

de Clé - ry, Ven - do - me, Ven - do - me.

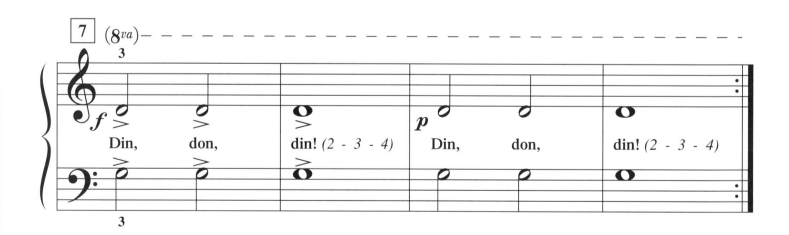

f Din, don, din! (2 - 3 - 4) p Din, don, din! (2 - 3 - 4)

FF1602

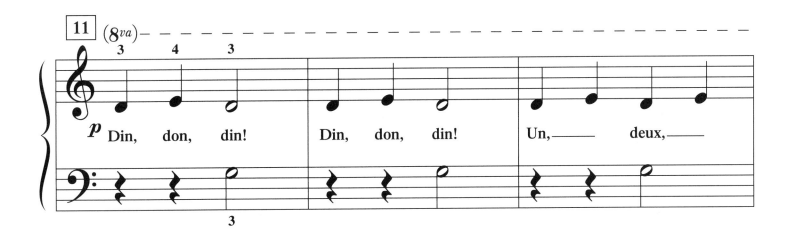

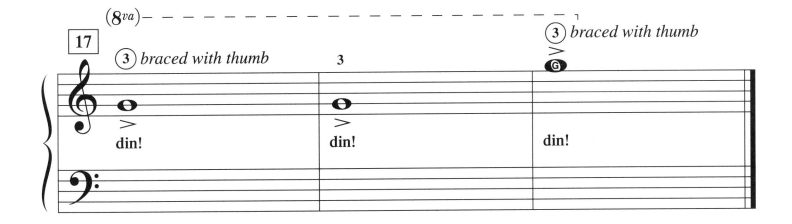

DISCOVERY

Where is there an echo in this piece?

Roller Skate Ride

Words by Crystal Bowman
Music by Nancy Faber

FF1602

DISCOVERY

Where do the *first* two lines of music appear later in the piece?

I Love Rain!

**Hold the damper pedal
down throughout the piece.**

Words by Jennifer MacLean
Music by Nancy Faber

Moderately

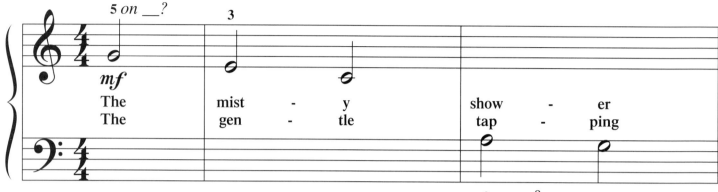

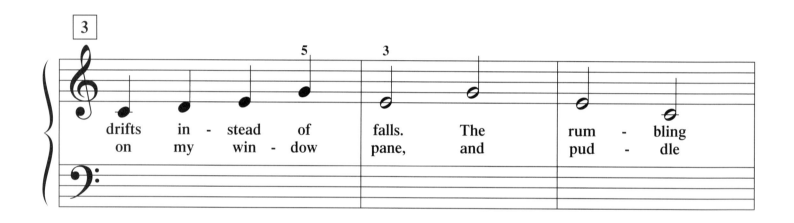

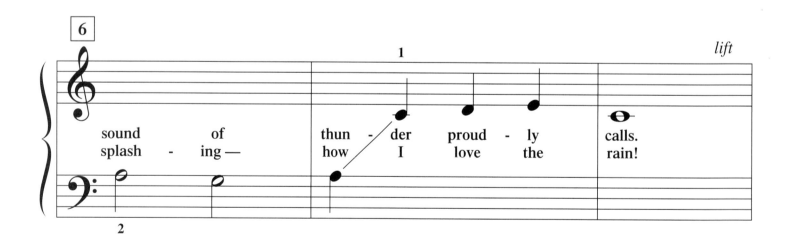

FF1602

Note: The teacher may teach this page through demonstration and pattern recognition.

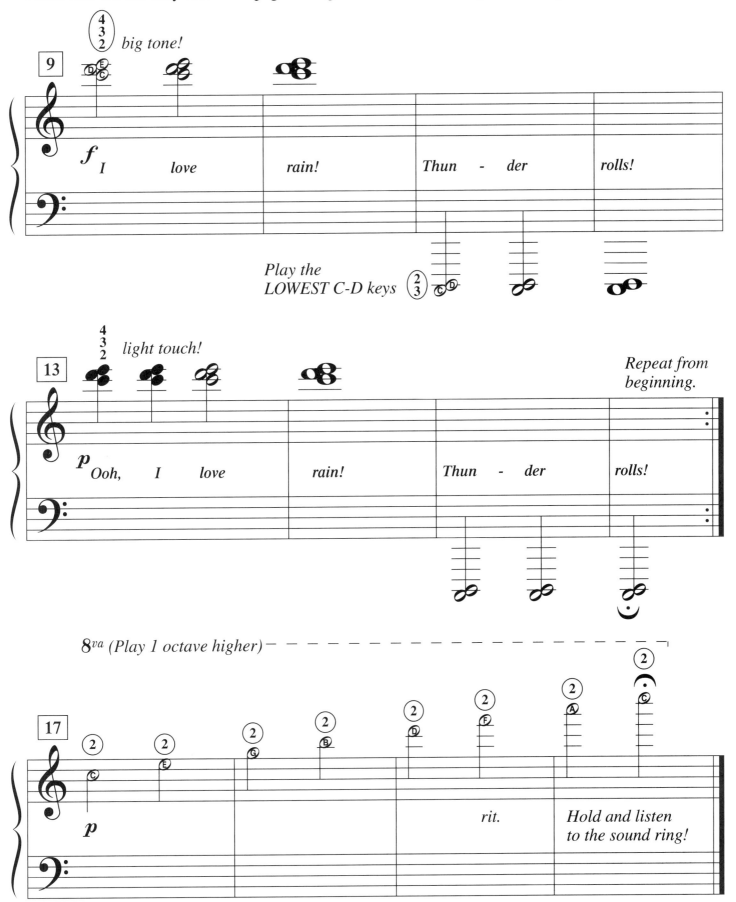

DISCOVERY

Does this piece end with **skips** or **steps**?

Chugging Choo-Choo

Your teacher will help you find the low L.H. position.
Listen for the great chug-a-lug sounds!

Words and Music
by Nancy Faber

With a great chug-a-lug beat

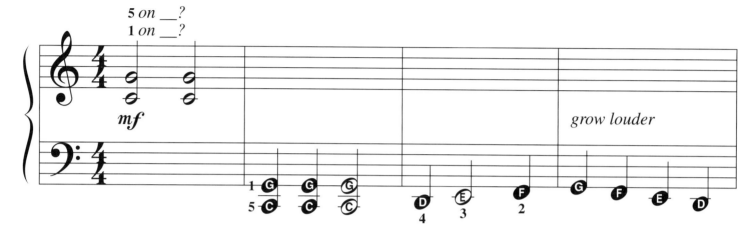

Hear the toot-in' choo-choo, chug-ging through the town. *(2 - 3 - 4)*

Chug, chug, choo-choo train, up hills and down a-gain. The

FF1602

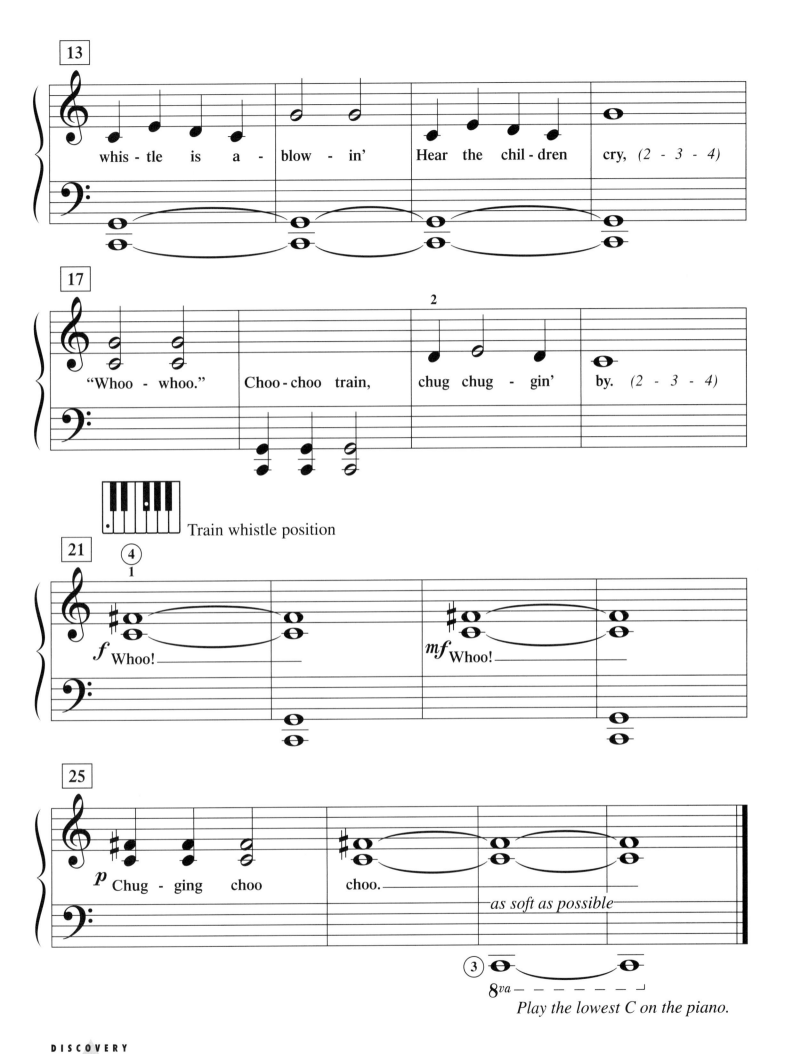

13 whis - tle is a - blow - in' Hear the chil - dren cry, *(2 - 3 - 4)*

17 "Whoo - whoo." Choo - choo train, **2** chug chug - gin' by. *(2 - 3 - 4)*

Train whistle position

21 ④ 1 *f* Whoo!_____ *mf* Whoo!_____

25 *p* Chug - ging choo choo._____ *as soft as possible*

③ *8va* — — — — — — ⌐

Play the lowest C on the piano.

DISCOVERY

Point out the following in this piece: *mezzo forte* sign, tie, step, skip, *piano* sign.

Eternally Music

Words by Jennifer MacLean
Music by Nancy Faber

Teacher Duet: (Student plays 1 octave higher)

FF1602

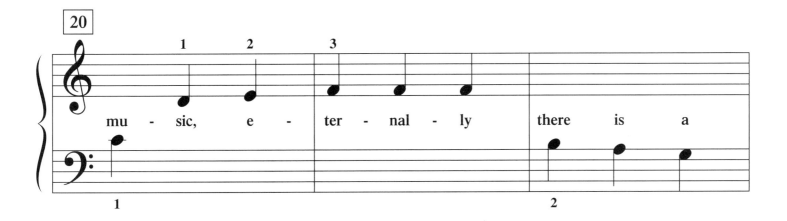

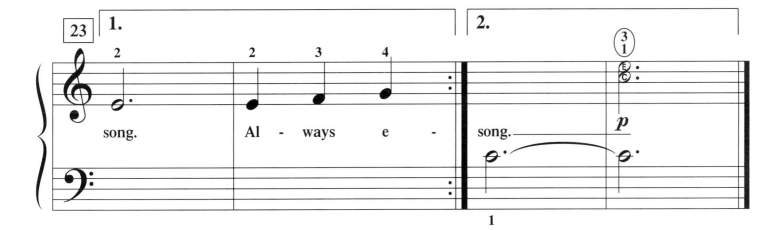

DISCOVERY

Explain the "roadmap" of this piece to your teacher.

Gold Star Dictionary

Circle a gold star when you can pronounce each term and tell your teacher what it means! Have fun listening to the Music Dicitonary Rap on the CD.

1.

accent

Play this note louder.

2.

a tempo

Return to the original tempo (speed).

3.

bass clef

Shows notes below Middle C. Also known as the F clef.

4.

dotted half note

3 beats. Count: 1-2-3.

5.

double bar line

The end of the piece.

6.

fermata

Hold this note longer.

7.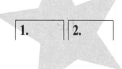

Play the 1st ending with repeat. Then play the 2nd ending, skipping over the 1st.

8.

Play 2 octaves higher or lower than written.

9.

flat

Play the nearest key to the left. (half step lower)

10. **ƒ**

forte

ƒ

Loud and strong.

11.

half note

2 beats. Count: 1-2.

12. *mf*

mezzo forte

mf

Moderately loud.

13.

8va

Play 1 octave higher or lower than written.

14. *p*
piano
Softly, gently.

15. *primo*
The higher part in a 4-hand duet.

16. quarter note
1 beat. Count: 1.

17. quarter rest
1 beat of silence.

18. repeat sign
Play once again.

19. *rit.* *ritardando* *ritard.*
Gradually play slower.

20. *secondo*
The lower part in a 4-hand duet.

21. sharp
Play the nearest key to the right. (half step higher)

22. tie
A curved line connecting the same notes. Hold for the total counts of both.

23. 4/4 3/4 time signature
Top number shows the number of beats per measure. Lower number shows the quarter note gets 1 beat.

24. treble clef
Shows notes above Middle C. Also known as the G clef.

25. whole note
4 beats. Count: 1-2-3-4.

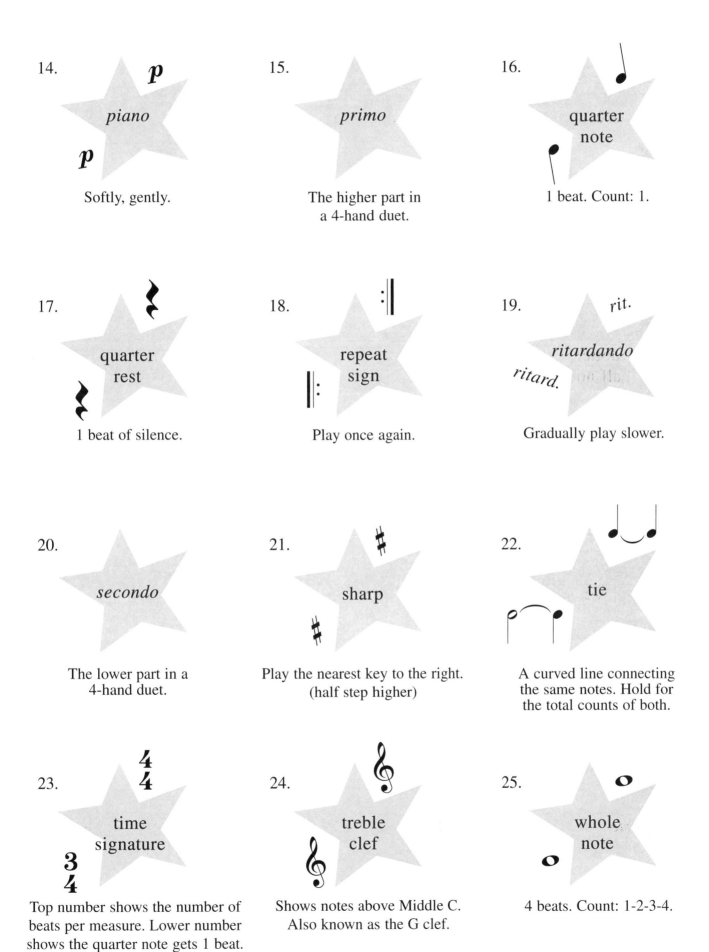

GOLD STAR CERTIFICATE

CONGRATULATIONS,
Gold Star Performer!

You have completed the Piano Adventures
Gold Star Performance, Primer Level.

You are now ready to begin
Gold Star Performance, Level 1.

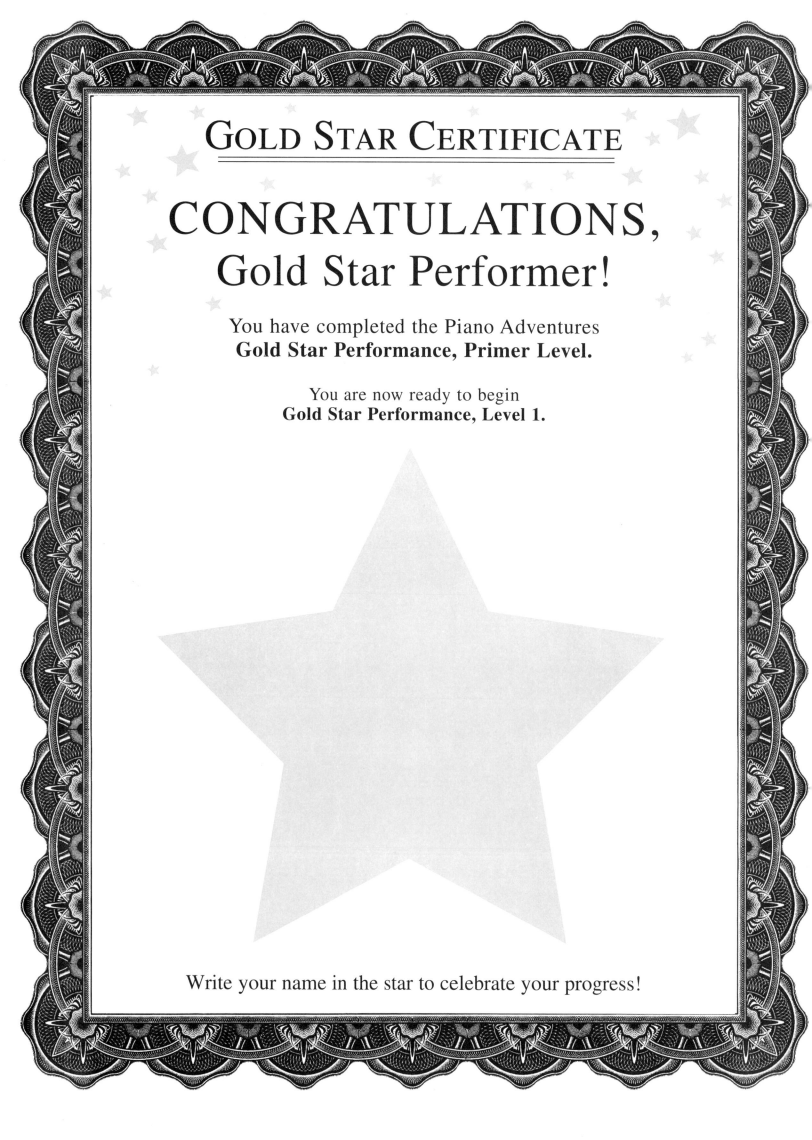

Write your name in the star to celebrate your progress!